ANIMAL MATH

Math and My World

Kieran Walsh

Rourke

Publishing LLC

Vero Beach, Florida 32964

www.rourkepublishing.com

PHOTO CREDITS:
All photos from AbleStock.com, except for page 5 by the author

Editor: Frank Sloan

Library of Congress Cataloging-in-Publication Data

Walsh, Kieran.
 Animal Math / Kieran Walsh.
     p. cm. -- (Math and my world)
 Includes bibliographical references and index.
 ISBN 1-59515-491-4 (hardcover)
 1. Arithmetic--Juvenile literature. 2. Animals--Juvenile literature. I.
Title.
 QA115.W268 2006
 513--dc22
                               2005014827

Printed in the USA

w/w

TABLE OF CONTENTS

INTRODUCTION

If you have ever visited a farm you know how important animals are. Animals provide us with food, teach us about our environment, and, in the case of pets, even keep us company.

As much as we might love them, though, animals are not human beings. They have different needs, and they even age differently.

For instance, imagine it's your birthday. One of the presents you are given is a brand new puppy. Five years after that, both you and your puppy would be five years older, right?

Yes and no. Five years have passed, but you and your puppy have aged differently. You see, dogs don't live as long as human beings do. On average, human beings in the United States live about 77 years. Dogs don't live that long. The number varies according to different breeds, but the average life expectancy for a dog is about 12 years.

What this means is that dogs age more quickly than humans do. People say that each dog year is about the same as 7 human years. If you do a little math, you can see where this idea came from:

$$7 \times 12 = 84$$

7 times 12 equals 84, which is slightly more than the life expectancy for a human.

This isn't quite accurate, though. For one thing, dogs do most of their growing in the first two years of their lives. In fact, the first two years of a dog's life are about the same as 21 years of a human's life. Meanwhile, every year after that is roughly equal to 4 human years.

So, if five years have passed, how many human years has your dog aged? You can find out in three steps:

$$2 \times 10.5 = 21 \text{ human years for}$$
the first 2 years of the dog's life…
$$3 \times 4 = 12 \text{ more human years…}$$
$$21 + 12 = 33$$

Your dog is about 33 human years old!

Because animals are important to us, we need to be able to understand them and care for them. In the following pages, you will see how math can help you.

Dogs age differently than humans do. In one human year, how much will this puppy age?

DINOSAURS

Dinosaurs were reptiles that existed during a period of Earth's history called the Mesozoic era. Scientists believe that the first dinosaurs appeared around 230 million years ago. Dinosaurs thrived for centuries, but they eventually became **extinct** around 65 million years ago.

How long did the dinosaurs live on Earth?

That might sound like a difficult question because the numbers are so big:

$$230{,}000{,}000 \qquad 65{,}000{,}000$$

Just to make things easier, drop the million:

$$230 \qquad 65$$

Now all you have to do is subtract the smaller number from the larger number:

$$230 - 65 = 165$$

The dinosaurs lived on Earth for about 165 million years!

Much of what we know about dinosaurs comes from the discovery and analysis of **fossils.** By assembling their skeletons, we can imagine what dinosaurs looked like and marvel at their size.

Dinosaur fossils found at Dinosaur Provincial Park in Canada

Not all dinosaurs were the same size, but the biggest dinosaurs were enormous. The largest type of dinosaur that has been discovered was a creature scientists have named the brachiosaur. The brachiosaur was about 75 feet long and 40 feet tall!

On the other hand, the smallest kind of dinosaur was called compsognathus. Compsognathus was only about 3 feet long.

How much longer was the brachiosaur compared to compsognathus?

Again, you can find the answer by using subtraction. Just subtract the smaller number from the larger number:

$$75 - 3 = 72$$

The brachiosaur was 72 feet longer than compsognathus!

No living person has ever actually seen a dinosaur, but by reconstructing their remains we can imagine what they looked like.

You may have seen movies where dinosaurs and humans interact. Human beings, though, were not in existence at the same time as the dinosaurs. Scientists estimate that the first creatures that we would recognize as human showed up about 6 million years ago.

How many years passed between the extinction of the dinosaurs and the arrival of humans? Remember that the dinosaurs died out around 65 million years ago.

$$65 - 6 = 59$$

About 59 million years!

What *if* human beings and dinosaurs had existed at the same time, though? How much bigger was the biggest dinosaur compared to a human being?

One thing to remember here is that the earliest humans were not as tall as people are now. Experts think that our oldest known ancestors may have been only about 4 feet tall. How does that compare to a brachiosaur?

$$40 - 4 = 36$$

A brachiosaur was about 36 feet taller than the earliest known human. Knowing that, you'll discover that it was probably a good thing dinosaurs and humans weren't on Earth at the same time!

Death of the Dinosaurs

One mystery about the dinosaurs that still remains unsolved is why they died out. Certainly their extinction was due to an extreme change in climate. The question is, what caused that change? Some scientists believe that an asteroid or maybe a series of comets hit the Earth and threw huge amounts of dirt into the air, blocking out the sunlight. Others believe that a number of volcanic explosions had a similar effect.

The collision of an asteroid with the planet Earth may have been the cause of the dinosaurs' extinction.

THE BLUE WHALE

The dinosaurs were big, but they weren't the biggest creatures ever. As a matter of fact, the biggest animal that ever lived on Earth is still in existence today.

The blue whale gets its name from its blue coloring. At birth, a blue whale is roughly 25 feet long. The average size of most adult blue whales is about 75 feet.

Several hundred times bigger than even the brachiosaur, the blue whale is probably the largest animal ever to exist.

How many feet does the average blue whale grow during its life?

$$75-25=50$$

A blue whale grows about 50 feet in its lifetime. Some fully grown blue whales, though, have reached a length of 100 feet! Let's compare that number with the size of the brachiosaur. If the brachiosaur was 75 feet long, how much bigger is the blue whale?

$$100 - 75 = 25$$

So, really huge blue whales can be up to 25 feet longer than the brachiosaur!

Comparing the brachiosaur and the blue whale is a bit unfair, though. For one thing, dinosaurs were land animals, while the blue whale lives in the water. What, then, is the biggest land animal?

The largest land animal in existence today is the African elephant. African elephants can grow up to 13 feet in height and weigh as much as 16,000 pounds.

Let's compare the African elephant with the brachiosaur. If the brachiosaur was 40 feet tall, how much taller was it than the African elephant?

$$40 - 13 = 27$$

The brachiosaur was about 27 feet taller than most elephants.

In terms of animals that are still around today, though, how do the blue whale and the African elephant compare?

The world's largest land animal, the African elephant

Obviously, the blue whale is longer than the African elephant. But instead, let's compare them in terms of weight. The heaviest blue whale ever captured weighed an incredible 389,760 pounds! The biggest elephant, on the other hand, weighed about 24,000 pounds:

$$389{,}760 - 24{,}000 = 365{,}760$$

Even the biggest elephant is outweighed by the biggest blue whale by about 365,000 pounds!

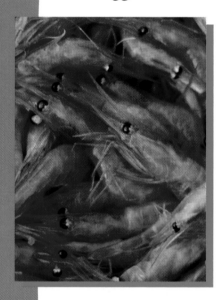

Believe it or not, these tiny krill are enough to feed the blue whale!

Krill

How much do you eat in one day? How much food do you think it would take to feed a creature the size of the blue whale?

In fact, the blue whale eats very small animals called krill. Krill are a bit like shrimp. They range in size from less than 1 inch to a little more than 5 inches long. In order for a blue whale to get enough food, it has to eat about 40 million krill every day!

Using multiplication, can you find out how many krill a blue whale eats in one week? In one year?

SPEED

So far, we've been dealing with animal height and weight. What makes an animal distinctive, though, isn't necessarily size.

Antelopes are the second fastest land animals on the planet. They can run at speeds up to 60 miles per hour.

Consider the cheetah. Cheetahs aren't very big. The typical adult cheetah is only about 4 feet long and weighs around 100 pounds. The cheetah, though, is the fastest land animal in the world. Cheetahs are capable of reaching top speeds of around 70 miles per hour. The African elephant has a top speed of only 25 miles per hour.

How much faster is the cheetah compared to the African elephant?

$$70 - 25 = 45$$

The cheetah is about 45 miles per hour faster than the African elephant. Just to put things in perspective, a cheetah would just about be able to keep up with a car traveling on a highway, while an African elephant would be left in the dust.

But the cheetah is not the fastest animal in the world. That honor belongs to the peregrine falcon. The peregrine falcon can fly at speeds up to 200 miles per hour. How much faster is the peregrine falcon compared to the cheetah?

$$200 - 70 = 130$$

The peregrine falcon is 130 miles per hour faster than the cheetah!

As you can see, we're starting to deal with some very big numbers. Saying that the peregrine falcon is 130 miles per hour faster than the cheetah is fine, but there is an easier way to express the same idea. You can do this by using **multiples.**

You may have noticed that the word "multiples" sounds a lot like *multiplication*. That's because any number being multiplied produces multiples. For instance, multiply the number 3 by some common **integers**:

$$0 \times 3 = 0$$
$$1 \times 3 = 3$$
$$2 \times 3 = 6$$

The answers 0, 3, and 6 are all multiples of 3!

Now consider these numbers:

$$4 \qquad 8$$

What would you have to multiply the number 4 by to give the product 8? You can find out by using division:

$$8 \div 4 = 2$$

Multiplying 4 by 2 gives 8. Another thing we can say here, though, is that the product 8 is *twice as much* as 4!

Let's apply this technique to the speeds of the falcon and the cheetah:

$$200 \div 70 = 2.85$$

And just to keep things simple, round that number up to 3. Now you can say that the falcon is about 3 *times faster* than the cheetah!

Remember the biggest animal in the world, the blue whale? The blue whale can only travel at around 30 miles per hour. Using the same technique, compare the blue whale with the falcon. Just divide the bigger number by the smaller number:

$$200 \div 30 = 6.66$$

And round the answer up to 7. The falcon is about 7 times faster than the blue whale!

If it traveled at 0.03 miles per hour, how long would it take this snail to cross from one side of your room to the other?

The Snail

With each of the examples we have looked at, you may have noticed that the animals' speed seems to increase as their size gets smaller. The cheetah is faster than the blue whale, and the falcon is faster than the cheetah. So the smaller the animal, the faster it is, right?

Not exactly. As it turns out, one of the slowest animals in the world is also one of the smallest. The snail travels only at 0.03 miles per hour! How could you express a comparison between the cheetah and the snail?

$$70 \div 0.03 = 2,333$$

The cheetah is more than 2,000 times faster than a snail!

ZOO ANIMALS

At some point in your life you have probably been to a zoo. Zoos are places where living animals are kept for people to look at and study. Some of the biggest zoos in the world are home to an incredible number of animals. The Bronx Zoo in New York houses around 4,000 animals. The London Zoo houses about 5,000 animals.

Zoos are the only opportunity most people will have to see animals from distant parts of the world.

Zoos include animals from all over the world. Not all of these animals can survive in the same conditions. Two extreme examples of this are gorillas and penguins.

Gorillas are huge animals that live mostly in the rain forests of **equatorial** Africa. Rain forests are generally warm places. The average temperature in a rain forest is about 80 degrees Fahrenheit, whether it is day or night. This is why zoo gorillas can be seen in outdoor habitats, at least during warm weather.

Penguins, on the other hand, are a kind of bird that can't fly. They spend most of their lives in the water and live in areas south of the equator. Many penguins live in warm climates, but the largest kind of penguin is the emperor penguin. Emperor penguins live on the coasts of Antarctica at the South Pole. Antarctica is the coldest place on earth. Average temperatures there hover around *minus* 58 degrees Fahrenheit! You can see now why penguins have to be kept in an indoor section of the zoo usually called a "bird house."

Most penguins are used to living in cold climates.

Let's say you're visiting a zoo with both a gorilla habitat and a bird house including penguins. It's early summer and the temperature is 75 degrees Fahrenheit.

How much warmer or cooler is it compared to the average temperature in the gorilla's natural habitat, the rain forest?

$$80 - 75 = 5$$

It is five degrees *cooler* than in the rain forest.

Now compare the outside temperature with the temperature that emperor penguins are used to. Remember that the average temperature in the Antarctic is minus 58 degrees. Another way of writing that number is:

$$^-58°F$$

What we're dealing with here is a **negative** number. Negative numbers are numbers with a value less than zero.

The important thing to remember is that all numbers, positive or negative, have an **absolute** value. To find out the absolute value of a number, just remove the sign. The absolute value of 5, for instance, is 5. The absolute value of ⁻5 is also 5. Likewise, the absolute value of ⁻58 is 58.

So, to answer the question, just add the external temperature to the absolute value of the temperature in the penguin house:

$$58 + 75 = 133$$

The temperature outside is 133 degrees Fahrenheit higher than in the penguin house!

American Rain Forests

A rain forest like the one African gorillas are used to living in might sound like a strange, exotic place. But really, a rain forest is just an area that receives a great deal of rain. Specifically, in order for an area to be a rain forest it has to receive at least 100 inches of rainfall per year. About how much rainfall does a rain forest receive in 8 years?

You might also be surprised to know that there are rain forests in the United States! One is the Hoh Rain Forest in Olympia, Washington. Another is the Kauai Rain Forest in Hawaii.

BABIES AND ADULTS

Many of the animals you can find at the zoo have more than one name. Did you know that a baby deer is called a fawn? A baby zebra, on the other hand, is called a colt.

Part of the reason why baby animals have different names from their adult versions is because they seem like completely different animals. For instance, lions are gigantic animals. A fully grown male lion can weigh as much as 400 pounds.

Here you can see the vast size difference between a baby giraffe and an adult giraffe. ▶

But, like all things big, the lion starts out very small. Baby lions are called cubs. When cubs are born they usually weigh less than 5 pounds.

Imagine an adult lion weighing 380 pounds. When this lion was born it weighed 3 pounds. How much weight did this lion gain during its lifetime?

This is an easy one. Just subtract the cub weight from the adult weight:

$$380 - 3 = 377$$

This lion gained 377 pounds in its lifetime. That's a lot of eating!

Another zoo animal with a different baby name is the giraffe. Baby giraffes are called calves. Even when they are born, calves are pretty big. The typical size of a calf is about 6 feet tall and it weighs roughly 125 pounds. That's bigger than some people!

But a calf still has a lot of growing to do before it becomes a giraffe. The average size for an adult giraffe is 18 feet tall, including a 7-foot-long neck. The average weight of an adult giraffe is 3,000 pounds.

Let's compare a calf with a fully grown giraffe. About how much weight does a giraffe gain during its lifetime?

$$3,000 - 125 = 2,875$$

A giraffe gains about 2,875 pounds in its lifetime!

What about height? How much taller is the average giraffe compared to a newborn calf?

$$18 - 6 = 12$$

A giraffe is about 12 feet taller than a calf!

Try something else. What if you wanted to complete this sentence? A giraffe is about ___ times bigger than a calf.

$$18 \div 6 = 3$$

A giraffe is about 3 times bigger than a calf!

Calves

"Calf" is actually a very common name for baby animals. You probably know that cows have babies named calves. Other species of animals with this baby name include:

Buffalo

Camels

Elephants

Hippopotamuses…and even Dolphins!

The hippopotamus is another animal that starts life as a "calf."

FISH

Of course, you don't have to go to a zoo to see animals. Some of your favorite animals might be living with you in your own home as pets. Any animal you take care of can be a pet. Just like zoo animals, though, pets are different from human beings and have different needs. Sometimes a pet's needs mean that the owner has to create a special **environment** for it.

One of the most common types of pet fish is the goldfish.

Fish are a good example of this. A person who wants to keep fish as pets will have to provide them with a special tank, or aquarium, that they can live in.

Fish are cold-blooded animals. This means that their body **temperature** changes depending on their environment. Goldfish are cold-water fish. They are comfortable in water that has a temperature between 68 and 72 degrees Fahrenheit. Tropical, or warm-water, fish require water with a temperature between 75 and 79 degrees Fahrenheit. This is why some aquariums need to have a water heater attached.

What is the difference in the water temperatures needed by cold-water fish and warm-water fish?

To find out the answer, you're going to have to calculate some averages. An **average** is a number that represents a group of numbers. The grades you get in school are averages. What if, during a grading period, your teacher gave you three tests and your scores for them were:

$$92$$
$$73$$
$$85$$

Based on these scores, what would your final grade be?

You can find out using two steps. First, add all the scores together:

$$92 + 73 + 85 = 250$$

Next, divide the result (250) by the number of addends. The **addends** are the numbers you added together. In this case, there were three addends, 92, 73, and 85:

$$250 \div 3 = 83.3$$

Your average grade with those test scores is 83.3! That's a B minus!

Using the same method, you can calculate the average temperature in an aquarium for cold-water fish. Remember that cold-water fish need water with a temperature between 68 and 72 degrees Fahrenheit.

$$68 + 72 = 140$$
$$140 \div 2 = 70$$

The ideal average water temperature for cold-water fish is 70 degrees Fahrenheit!

Many fish owners line their aquariums with pebbles and plants to give their pets a home more like the ocean.

Now calculate the average water temperature for warm-water fish. Warm-water fish need water that has a temperature between 75 and 79 degrees Fahrenheit.

$$75 + 79 = 154$$
$$154 \div 2 = 77$$

Ideally, warm-water fish need water that has an average temperature of 77 degrees Fahrenheit!

So now that you have both averages, what is the *difference* between the water temperature for cold-water fish and the water temperature for warm-water fish?

$$77 - 70 = 7$$

Warm-water fish need water with a temperature about 7 degrees warmer than cold-water fish!

Aquariums can be as small as a coffee table or the size of entire buildings.

Aquariums

A zoo is where you can see a variety of animals from around the world all in one place. In order to see fish from around the world in one place, though, you go to an aquarium. In an aquarium, the natural environments of different species of fish are recreated so that they can be watched.

These aquariums, of course, are much bigger than the ones someone might keep at home. Imagine that you own an aquarium that holds 10 gallons of water. How does that compare to the Virginia Marine Science Museum, which has a number of tanks holding a total of about 800,000 gallons of water?

ENDANGERED SPECIES

We have spent a lot of time looking at different kinds of animals and their needs. All this should give you some idea of how delicate animals are. If they don't live in the right environment, or if their environment suddenly changes, they can become sick and even die out—just like the dinosaurs did.

When an entire species of animal dies out they are said to be **extinct**. Animal species that are in danger of becoming extinct are **endangered**.

One of the most famous endangered animals is the bald eagle. Before the first Europeans settled in America, it is believed that the bald eagle population numbered as high as 500,000. By 1963, the population of Bald Eagles was only about 800.

The bald eagle is one of the most common symbols of the United States. Since 1782, a picture of this animal has appeared on each and every one of the dollar bills circulating in America. ▶

By 1963, how much had the bald eagle population decreased?

$$500,000 - 800 = 499,200$$

The bald eagle population had decreased by 499,200.

The bald eagle was first listed as an endangered species in 1967. Assuming that it is 2006 when you read this, for how many years has the bald eagle been listed as an endangered species?

$$2006 - 1967 = 39$$

The bald eagle has been listed as an endangered species for 39 years.

Due to the efforts of wildlife organizations and **conservation** agencies, the population of bald eagles has grown significantly in recent years. This means that the bald eagle may even be removed from the list of endangered species. As of 2002, the number of bald eagles in the United States numbered about 12,000.

Using the 2002 population number, can you calculate how much the bald eagle population has increased since 1963?

$$12,000 - 800 = 11,200$$

Since 1963, the bald eagle population has increased by 11,200!

11,200 is a very big number, though. To make things easier, maybe you could express the population increase in terms of multiples.

To start with, look at the numbers again:

12,000 800

12,000 is the larger number, which means that it is a multiple of 800. In other words, 800 multiplied by *something* will produce 12,000:

$$800 \times ? = 12{,}000$$

This might look like a difficult task at first, but to find out the answer, all you need to do is rearrange some of the numbers and turn the multiplication problem into a division problem:

$$? = 12{,}000 \div 800$$
$$12{,}000 \div 800 = 15$$

So, 800 multiplied by 15 gives us 12,000. This means that the 2002 population of bald eagles in the United States was 15 *times greater* than it was in 1963! That's good news for both bald eagles and human beings.

Pesticides are dangerous, but they are only one of the threats to our environment. Others include various forms of pollution like litter and acid rain.

Pesticides

The massive decrease in the bald eagle population during the 20th Century was due to a number of factors, but mainly because of the use of the **pesticide** DDT.

Pesticides are chemicals used to kill insects that are harmful to people. DDT was a pesticide that originally came into use in the 1940s. After the decrease in population of a number of different species of wildlife, though, DDT use was banned in the United States in 1972.

CONCLUSION

If you really love animals, maybe you will become a **veterinarian** when you grow up. A veterinarian is a person responsible for the medical care of animals. Veterinarians use math every day to determine if the animals they examine are sick or healthy. Maybe you'd even like to work in a zoo with a specific type of animal like monkeys or snakes.

You may have to wait a little while to become a veterinarian, though. Most people enter veterinary school around the age of 18.

How many years do you have to wait until you can start studying to become a veterinarian?

Maybe you can be a veterinarian!

THE METRIC SYSTEM

We actually have two systems of weights and measures in the United States. Quarts, pints, gallons, ounces, and pounds are all units of the U.S. Customary System, also known as the English System.

The other system of measurement, and the only one sanctioned by the United States Government, is the metric system, which is also known as the International System of Units. French scientists developed the metric system in the 1790s. The basic unit of measurement in the metric system is the meter, which is about one ten-millionth the distance from the North Pole to the equator.

A metal bar used to represent the length of the standard meter was even created. This bar was replaced in the 1980s, though, when scientists changed the standard of measurement for the meter to a portion of the distance traveled by light in a vacuum.

The metric system can be applied to the world of animals in a number of different ways. For instance, we looked at the speeds of different kinds of animals, including the world's fastest land animal, the cheetah. The cheetah can reach a top speed of 70 miles per hour. In the metric system, though, speed is measured not in miles, but in kilometers.

One mile is equal to 1.621 kilometers. How fast can a cheetah travel in terms of kilometers?

Since you already know the top speed of a cheetah in miles, you can find out by using multiplication:

$$70 \times 1.621 = 113.47$$

A cheetah can run at about 113 kilometers per hour!

Another instance where you can apply the metric system to the world of animals is temperature. When measuring temperature, most of the world does not use the Fahrenheit system. Instead, they rely on the Celsius Scale, which treats the freezing point of water as 0 degrees and the boiling point of water as 100 degrees.

Converting a Fahrenheit temperature to a Celsius temperature is fairly simple. Just subtract 32 from the Fahrenheit temperature and then divide the result by 1.8.

Let's apply this to the example of a tank meant for warm-water fish. Ideally, warm-water fish need water with an average temperature of 77 degrees Fahrenheit. What would the ideal temperature be on the Celsius Scale?

$$77 - 32 = 45$$
$$45 \div 1.8 = 25$$

On the Celsius Scale, the ideal water temperature for warm-water fish is 25 degrees Celsius!

As you can see, the metric system is pretty easy once you get the hang of it. For practice, you could go through this book and convert some of the numbers to metric.

Try it!

Iguanas need an environment with a temperature around 90 degrees Fahrenheit. What is that in degrees Celsius?

GLOSSARY

absolute — the pure value of a number, regardless of whether it is positive or negative

addends — the numbers added together in an addition problem

average — a number used to represent a group of numbers

conservation — the protection of natural resources and wildlife

endangered — in danger of becoming extinct

environment — the habitat or living area of an animal

equatorial — in the area of the equator

extinct — no longer existing

fossils — traces of plants or animals that lived millions of years ago, that are preserved in rocks

integers — numbers

multiples — the result of multiplying a single number by a series of other numbers

negative — with a value less than zero

pesticide — chemicals used to kill insects

temperature — the measure of hotness or coldness for an environment

veterinarian — a doctor who cares for animals

Further Reading

Slavin, Steve. *All the Math You'll Ever Need*. John Wiley and Sons, Inc. 1999.

Zeman, Anne and Kate Kelly. *Everything You Need To Know About Math Homework*. Scholastic, 1994.

Zeman, Anne and Kate Kelly. *Everything You Need to Know About Science Homework*. Scholastic, 1994.

Websites to Visit

http://science.howstuffworks.com/question687.htm
How Stuff Works – "What is the biggest animal ever to exist on earth?"

http://pubs.usgs.gov/gip/dinosaurs/sizes.html
U.S. Geological Survey – "What Was the Biggest Dinosaur? What Was the Smallest?"

http://www.worldalmanacforkids.com/explore/animals2.html
World Almanac for Kids – Fastest Animals

http://www.fws.gov/
U.S. Fish and Wildlife Service

INDEX

ABOUT THE AUTHOR

Kieran Walsh has written a variety of children's nonfiction books, primarily on historical and social studies topics, including the Rourke series *Holiday Celebrations* and *Countries in the News*. He lives in New York City.